Carly Simon

ISBN 978-1-4803-5094-6

HAL•LEONARD®
CORPORATION

7777 W. BLUEMOUND RD. P.O.BOX 13819 MILWAUKEE, WI 53213

Visit Hal Leonard Online at
www.halleonard.com

Guitar Chord Songbook

Contents

All I Want Is You

Words and Music by Carly Simon,
Jacob Brackman and Andy Goldmark

Melody:

What do the neigh - bors say

(Capo 1st fret)

Cadd9   Gadd2   Em7   D/E   D   D/C   C   D/A

Am7   A/B   Gmaj7   A   Cmaj9   G   G/D   Bm

A/G   E   B/C#   Amaj7   B   F#m7

Intro ‖: **Cadd9** | | **Gadd2** | :‖

Verse 1

    Em7   **D/E**   **Em7**
What do the neighbors say

         D
When they hear us scream at night?

        Em7 **D/E** **Em7**
Do they talk a - bout a love

      D
All ____ in tatters?

Em7   **D/E**   **Em7**
What do the neighbors know

     D
A - bout the heart and soul,

     Em7 **D/E**   **Em7**
The fire   down be - low

     D
That real - ly matters?

         D/C C
They can nev - er guess

         D/A Am7
In the si - lences

Chorus 1

      D   **A/B**
That all I want is you

        Gmaj7   **A**   **Em7**
And the sexy hurricane ___ we got here.

D   **A/B**
All I want is you.

        Gmaj7   **A**
I don't want a man who says,

                Em7
"Good morning, dear." No, no.

  Cmaj9   **G**
All ___ I want is you, all that I want ___ is you.

  Cmaj9   **G**
All ___ I want is you, nobody else ___ but you.

Verse 2

        Em7 D/E Em7
Let 'em listen at the door.

        D
Let 'em listen through the floor.

        Em7 D/E   **Em7**
Let 'em go a - head and draw

           D
The wrong ___ conclusions.

      Em7   **D/E**   **Em7**
So chase me 'round the room,

         D
Make me crazy like the moon.

Pre-Chorus 2   *Repeat Pre-Chorus 1*

Chorus 2

D   A/B
That all I want is you

     Gmaj7   A   Em7
And the sexy hurricane ____ that we share.

D   A/B
All I want is you.

     Gmaj7   A
I don't want a man who tip - toes up the stairs.

     Em7
No, I don't.

    Cmaj9   G
All ____ I want is you, all that I want ____ is you.

    Cmaj9   G
All ____ I want is you, nobody else ____ but you.

Instrumental

| G/D   D | | A/B | Bm |
| Gmaj7 A/G G | | A | |

Pre-Chorus 3

      D/C C   A
They'll nev - er guess in the silences

Outro-Chorus

     E   B/C♯
That all I want is you

     Amaj7   B
And the sexy hurricane ____ that we share.

     F♯m7 E   B/C♯
Oh, babe, _____ all I want is you.

     Amaj7   B
I don't want a man who tip - toes up the stairs.

       F♯m7
He's gonna fall.

E   B/C♯
All I want is you

     Amaj7   B
And your freight train whistling o - ver my track.

     F♯m7 E   B/C♯
Oh, babe, _____ all I want is you

     Amaj7   B
And your Mack truck love jump - ing me, Jack.

     F♯m7 E   B/C♯
Oh Jack, _____ all I want is you…   ***Fade out***

Attitude Dancing

Words and Music by
Carly Simon and Jacob Brackman

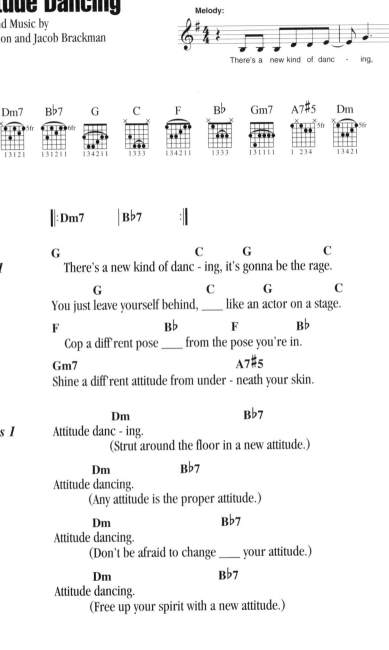

Melody:

There's a new kind of danc - ing,

Dm7 Bb7 G C F Bb Gm7 A7#5 Dm

Intro

‖: Dm7 | Bb7 :‖

Verse 1

G   C   G   C
There's a new kind of danc - ing, it's gonna be the rage.

G   C   G   C
You just leave yourself behind, ___ like an actor on a stage.

F   Bb   F   Bb
Cop a diff'rent pose ___ from the pose you're in.

Gm7   A7#5
Shine a diff'rent attitude from under - neath your skin.

Chorus 1

                    Dm   Bb7
Attitude danc - ing.
            (Strut around the floor in a new attitude.)

            Dm   Bb7
Attitude dancing.
      (Any attitude is the proper attitude.)

            Dm   Bb7
Attitude dancing.
      (Don't be afraid to change ___ your attitude.)

            Dm   Bb7
Attitude dancing.
      (Free up your spirit with a new attitude.)

Verse 2

```
       G              C   G              C
   It don't really mat - ter if you stretch or shake.

       G            C        G              C
   And it don't really mat - ter what moves your body makes.

       F            Bb       F              Bb
   And it don't really mat - ter what steps you choose to do.

   Gm7                              A7#5
   Only one thing matters, and that your attitude, (Attitude.) your attitude.
```

Chorus 2

```
          Dm               Bb7
   Attitude dancing.
          (Strut around the floor in a new attitude.)

          Dm               Bb7
   Attitude dancing.
          (Learn to move in an - other attitude.)

          Dm               Bb7
   Attitude dancing.
          (Find the groove in a new attitude.)

          Dm               Bb7
   Attitude dancing.
          (Don't be afraid of a new attitude.)
```

Guitar Solo

```
   ‖: G      | C      | G      | C      :‖
```

Verse 3

```
       F            Bb       F              Bb
   But it don't really mat - ter what steps you choose to do.

   Gm7                        A7#5
   The only thing that matters is your atti - tude, (Attitude.) your attitude.
```

Chorus 3

       Dm   B♭7
Attitude dancing.
           (Strut around the floor in a new attitude.)

  Dm   B♭7
(Do the locomotion in a new attitude.)

  Dm   B♭7
(Do the mashed potato in a new attitude.)

  Dm   B♭7
(Do the hully gully in a new attitude.)

Verse 4

  G   C   G   C
  Find a role you like, ___ we'll capture it, and freeze.

         G   C   G   C
Well, then turn it around ___ hundred and eighty degrees.

  F   B♭   F   B♭
Or if you're at a loss ___ just ob - serve some nat'ral dude,

  Gm7   A7♯5
Turn into a mirror of his atti - tude, (Attitude.) his attitude.

       Dm   B♭7 Dm B♭7
Attitude dancing.

Instrumental   ‖: Dm | B♭7 | Dm | B♭7   :‖ *Play 3 times*

Outro-Chorus   *Repeat Chorus 1 w/ Vocal ad lib.*

Anticipation

Words and Music by
Carly Simon

Melody:

We _____ can nev-er know

D D7sus4 G Em7 Asus4 A Dsus4 Dmaj7 A7 G6/D

Intro

| D   D7sus4 | D | |

Verse 1

D   G   D
We can never know about the days to come,

                  G   Em7 Asus4 A
But we think ____ about them any-way.

              D   G   D
And I wonder if I'm really with ____ you now,

              G   Em7 A   D   D7sus4   D
Or just chasing after some fin   -   er day.

Chorus 1

G   Dmaj7
  Anticipation,   anticipation

Em7   A   Em7   A
Is making me late, is keeping me waiting.

Verse 2

       D   G   D
And I tell you how easy it feels to be with you.

                        G   Em7   Asus4 A
How right your arms ___ feel around me.

       D   G   D
But I, I re-hearsed these words just late ___ last night

            G   Em7   A   D D7sus4 D
When I was thinking about how right tonight ___ might be.

Chorus 2   *Repeat Chorus 1*

Verse 3

         D   G   D
And to-morrow we might not be to-gether,

                      G   Em7   Asus4 A
I'm no prophet and I don't know nature's ways.

       D   G   D
So I'll try and see into your eyes ___ right now,

      G   Em7   A7   D
And stay right here, 'cause these are the good old days.

       G6/D D
These are the good old days.

      G   Em7   A7   D
And stay right here, 'cause these are the good old days.

       G6/D D   G6/D D
These are the good old days. These are the good old days.

       G6/D D   G6/D N.C.   D
These are the good old days. These are   the good old days.

Back Down to Earth

Words and Music by
Carly Simon

Melody:

We jumped in - to a riv-er on ___ the moon

Chords: Am7, D, G, Gsus4, Em7, Bm7, C, G*, Dsus2, A7, F, F/C

Intro

| Am7 D | G Gsus4 G | Am7 D | Em7 Bm7 |

Verse 1

C   G*
We jumped into a river on the moon

   C   G*
But the water was too cold.

C   G* Em7
We tried to buy the morn - ing star

Am7   Dsus2 D
But it was already sold.

Pre-Chorus 1

Em7   A7
I wanted to make it big ___ with you

     Em7   A7
But my plans ___ must have been too bold.

Chorus 1

    Am7   D   G*
And it's back down to earth again.

C   D   Em7
Back in my car ___ and gone.

Am7   F
Back on the road,

Am7   D   G*
Back on the road alone.

Verse 2

```
C                    G*
  You were my summer angel

    C            G*
Your eyes how they ___ shone.

C                    G*        Em7
Just last night we were talk - ing about

          Am7                Dsus2  D
How much ___ our love had grown.
```

Pre-Chorus 2

```
 Em7              A7
I wanted to prove how good it could be

          Em7                     A7
But my plans ___ will have to be postponed.
```

Chorus 2

```
          Am7       D      G*
'Cause it's back down to earth again.

        C        D        Em7
Back ___ in my car ___ and gone.

Am7       F
Back on the road,

    Am7            D      G*
Back ___ on the road ___ alone.
```

Guitar Solo

```
| C        | G*       | C       | G*      |
| C        | G* Em7   | Am7     | D       |
```

Pre-Chorus 3

Em7   A7
I wanted to prove just how good it could be

    Em7   A7
But my plans ___ will have to be postponed.

Chorus 3

    Am7   D G*
'Cause it's back down to earth again.

   C   D   Em7
Back ___ in my car ___ and gone.

Am7   F
Back on the road,

  Am7   D G*
Back ___ on the road ___ alone.

Am7   D G*
Back down to earth again.

   C   D   Em7
Back ___ in my car ___ and gone.

Am7   F
Back on the road,

Am7   D G*   F/C C G*
Back on the road ___ a - lone.

Better Not Tell Her

Words and Music by
Carly Simon

Melody:

Bet-ter not tell ___ her

F#m7add4 C#7 F#m7 D D/E G Gsus4

Intro

‖: F#m7add4 | | | :‖

Verse 1

F#m7add4   C#7   F#m7add4
Better not tell her   that I was your lov - er.

            C#7   F#m7add4
Better not make her   jealous of me.

              C#7   F#m7add4
Mm, better convince her   there was nothing between ___ us.

                C#7 F#m7
I'm not those initials in your diary.

Pre-Chorus 1

        D   D/E
But if you slip and my name ___ comes up,

        D   D/E
Don't deny that you knew ___ me.

Chorus 1

        G   Gsus4 G
Just leave out the white nights,

        D
The moon in your window,

        G   Gsus4 G
The break in your whisper,

        D   G   Gsus4 G   D
The promises after.

Verse 2

F#m7add4   C#7   F#m7add4
 Better not tell her why you love Spanish danc - ing.

         C#7   F#m7add4
Don't bother to say that it's hot in the summer in Madrid.

     C#7   F#m7add4
Let it all go now like smoke from a can - dle,

        C#7   F#m7
Like the trace of a song ___ that you hear in the wind.

Pre-Chorus 2

       D   D/E
But if you ___ slip and my name ___ should come up,

       D   D/E
Don't deny that you once knew me.

Chorus 2

       G   Gsus4 G
Just leave out the white nights,

       D
The moon in your window,

       G   Gsus4 G
The break in your whisper,

       D
The promises after.

         G   Gsus4 G
Leave out the tears and the laughter,

       D
She won't need to know

       G   Gsus4 G   D
That I cried when you left,   that I think of you still.

Guitar Solo 1 ‖: F#m7add4 | | C#7 | F#m7add4 :‖

Pre-Chorus 3

         D   D/E
But if you ____ slip and my name ____ comes up,

         D   D/E
Don't deny that you once ____ knew me.

Chorus 3

         G   Gsus4 G
Just leave out the white nights,

         D
The moon in your window,

         G   Gsus4 G
The break in your whisper,

         D
The promises after.

                G   Gsus4 G
Leave out the tears and the laughter,

         D   G
She won't need to know that I'd have died for your love.

Gsus4 G   D
          That I still love you.

Guitar Solo 2

| G | | | D | | | |

Chorus 4

G   Gsus4 G
Leave out the white nights,

        D
The moon in your window.

G   Gsus4 G
Leave out the white nights,

        D
The promises after.

 G   Gsus4 G D
‖: Leave out the white nights.   :‖ *Play 4 times*

Outro

| G Gsus4 G | Gsus4 G | D | | ‖

Back the Way

from the Motion Picture
THIS IS MY LIFE

Words and Music by
Carly Simon

Melody:
Back the way it was be - fore,

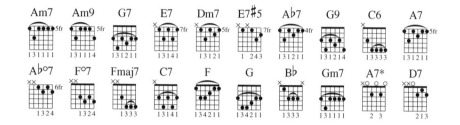

| Am7 | Am9 | G7 | E7 | Dm7 | E7#5 | A♭7 | G9 | C6 | A7 |
| Amo7 | F°7 | Fmaj7 | C7 | F | G | B♭ | Gm7 | A7* | D7 |

Intro |Am7 Am9 Am7 Am9 |Am7 G7 |Am7 |E7 |

Verse 1

      Am7   Dm7
   Back the way it was before,

      E7   Am7
Be - fore the door was o - pened,

           Dm7
Back the way it was before

       E7   E7#5 E7 Am7
Be - fore the ice _____ was broken.

        A♭7 G7   G9   C6
Back the   way it used to be

  A7   Dm7
Ev'ryone thought I was funny

     A♭°7 F°7 C6
But nobody ever asked me

        Fmaj7   G7   C7
If I wanted tiny little sandwiches sent up to my room.

Verse 2

Am7   Dm7   E7   Am7
Back the way it was before I was always waiting,

             Dm7   E7   Am7
Ev'ryone thought I was okay, but now I'm scintil - lating.

    A♭7 G7   G9   C6
Back the   way it used to be

A7   Dm7
Some people thought I was pretty

   F°7   A♭°7   C6
But not many pass - es were made at me

      G7   C6
Back the way it was be - fore.

Bridge 1

Dm7
But now my prayers are answered

     F   G
And my star is on the rise.

B♭   Gm7
Flashbulbs popping, traffic stopping,

F   A7* D7
Ev'ryone's my best ____ friend.

Verse 3

Am7   Dm7   E7 E7♯5 E7 Am7
Back the way it used to be.

              Dm   E7 E7♯5 E7 Am7
Back the way it used to be.

      G7   C6
Back the way it used to be

A7   Dm7
Money was always a ty - rant.

   A♭°7   F°7   C6
I spent it all paying my rent

      G7   C6
Back the way it used to be.

Bridge 2   *Repeat Bridge 1*

Outro

Am7
‖: Back the way

Dm7   E7 E7♯5 E7 Am7
It used to be.   :‖ ***Repeat and fade***
                                      w/ vocal ad lib.

Boys in the Trees

Words and Music by
Carly Simon

Melody:

I'm home a - gain _____ in

Chord diagrams: E9sus4, Bm7add4, D/G, D/F#, Esus4, G, Gsus4, F#m7♭5, Bm7, Cmaj9, Cmaj7, F#sus4, F#, C#m7♭5, E, A/C#, D, G7, F#m7, B7, D6/F#

Intro

| E9sus4 | | | | |

| Bm7add4 | | D/G | | |

| Bm7add4 | | D/G | | D/F# |

Verse 1

Esus4   G   Gsus4 G
I'm home again in my old narrow bed

Esus4   G
Where I grew tall and my feet hung over the end.

  F#m7♭5   Bm7   Cmaj9
The low beam room with a window looking out

     G   Cmaj7
On the soft summer gar - den

    F#sus4 F#   Bm7add4
Where the boys   grew in the trees.

Verse 2

Esus4   G
Here I grew guilty and no one was at fault.

Esus4   G
Frightened by the power in ev'ry innocent thought

   F#m7♭5   Bm7   Cmaj9
And the silent understand - ing passing down

     G   Cmaj7
From daughter to daughter.

    F#sus4 F#   D/G   C#m7♭5 Bm7
Let the boys   grow in the trees. (Boys in the trees.)

Verse 3

Esus4   G
Do you go to them or do you let them come to you?

Esus4   G
Do you stand in back afraid ___ that you'll intrude,

F#m7b5   Bm7   Cmaj9
De - ny yourself and hope ___ someone will see,

G   Cmaj7
And live like a flow - er

F#sus4 F#   Bm7
While the boys   grow in the trees?

Bridge

C#m7b5 Bm7 Esus4 E
(La, la, la, ___ la, la.)

A/C#   D   G7
(La, la, la, la, la. ___ La, la, la, la, la.)

F#m7   B7
(La, la, la, la, la, la, la, la, la.)

Verse 4

Esus4   G
Last night I slept in sheets the color of fire.

Esus4   G
To - night I lie alone again and I curse my own desires.

F#m7b5   Bm7   Cmaj9
Sentenced first to burn ___ and then to freeze

G   Cmaj7
And watch by the win - dow

F#sus4 F#   Bm7
Where the boys   grew in the trees.

F#sus4 F#   Bm7add4   D/G
The boys   grew in the trees.
(Boys in the trees.)

| Bm7add4 | | | D/G | | D6/F# | E9sus4 ‖

Coming Around Again
from the Paramount Picture HEARTBURN

Words and Music by
Carly Simon

Melody:

Ba - by sneez - es, _____

C   Am7   Fsus2   F   Dm   B♭sus2

F/E♭   E♭   Cm6   D/C   F/A   C/E

Intro

| C | | | Am7 | | |
| Fsus2 | | | C | | |

Verse 1

C   Am7
  Baby sneezes,   Mommy pleases,

Fsus2   C
  Daddy breezes in.

                   Am7
So good on paper,   so romantic,

Fsus2   C
  But so bewildering.

Chorus 1

     F   Dm
  I know nothing stays the same,

                          B♭sus2
But if you're willing to play the game,

                 F
It's coming around again.

     F/E♭ E♭   Cm6 D/C
So don't mind if I fall a - part,

        F/A   C/E
There's more room in a broken heart.

Verse 2

C   Am7
 You pay the grocer, you fix the toaster,

Fsus2   C
 You kiss the host goodbye.

         Am7
Then you break a window, burn the soufflé,

Fsus2   C
 Scream the lullaby.

Chorus 2   *Repeat Chorus 1*

Verse 3

C   Am7
 And I believe in love.

        Fsus2
But what else can I do?

       C
I'm so in love with you.

Chorus 3

F   Dm
 I know nothing stays the same,

          B♭sus2
But if you're willing to play the game,

         F
It will be coming around again.

      Dm
 Baby sneezes, Mommy pleases,

B♭sus2   F
 Daddy breezes in.

Outro-Chorus

  F   Dm
‖: I know nothing stays the same,

          B♭sus2
But if you're willing to play the game,

         F
It will be coming around again.

I do believe, I do believe,

Dm   B♭sus2
I believe in love. I believe in love

F
Coming around again, coming around again. :‖ ***Repeat and fade***
                   w/ vocal ad lib.

Darkness Till Dawn

Words and Music by
Carly Simon and Jacob Brackman

Melody:

Chain-smok-in' cig-a-rettes, _

A   G   Em7   F#m7   Bm7   F   Dm7   C   D   G7

Verse 1

      A   G
      Chain-smokin' cigarettes, enemies across the table.

Em7   F#m7   Bm7
Wonderin' if I can ever trust anyone ___ again.

A   G
We argue through the night, the restaurant shuts, you catch your flight,

  Em7   F#m7   Bm7
I ___ hail a cab with no idea where home might be.

Chorus 1

      A   G
      We both believed my chance ___ was gone,

      F   Dm7
But ain't it strange how life ___ goes on.

     C   D
A storm can never rage ___ forever,

      G   G7   C   D C D
And darkness only lasts till dawn.

Verse 2

```
A                      G
    Hotel blinds stay drawn. Nothin' seems to make me care.

Em7                F#m7    Bm7
I can't find a reason to comb my hair.

A                      G
Folks walkin' in the street, ev - 'ryone has something to do.

Em7                          F#m7        Bm7
My brain won't stop showing those old movies of you.
```

Chorus 2   *Repeat Chorus 1*

Verse 3

```
A                      G
    Weeks pass and your voice ____ sounds strange on the telephone.

Em7                          F#m7      Bm7
Strange how smooth and casual my own ____ voice sounds.

A                  G
I find that I'm list'ning to a tune comin' over my radio.

  Em7                          F#m7  Bm7
It makes me think of a guy I knew a while ago,

  F#m7    Bm7   F#m7   Bm7
A while ago, ____ a while ago.

| A       | G       | F       | Dm7       |
```

Outro

```
  C                  D
A storm can never rage ____ forever

  G           G7    C   D
And darkness only lasts till dawn.

    C  D        C  D        C  D
Oh, ____ oh, oh, oh, ____ oh, oh, oh.
```

Davy

Words and Music by
Carly Simon

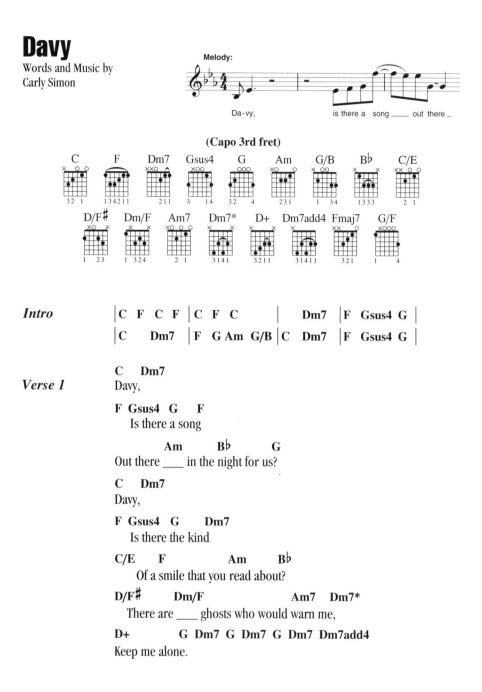

Melody:

Da-vy,   is there a song ___ out there

(Capo 3rd fret)

Intro	C F C F	C F C		Dm7	F Gsus4 G

	C Dm7	F G Am G/B	C Dm7	F Gsus4 G

Verse 1

      C   Dm7
Davy,

     F Gsus4 G   F
   Is there a song

            Am   B♭   G
Out there ___ in the night for us?

      C   Dm7
Davy,

     F Gsus4 G   Dm7
   Is there the kind

      C/E   F   Am   B♭
   Of a smile that you read about?

      D/F♯   Dm/F   Am7   Dm7*
   There are ___ ghosts who would warn me,

      D+   G Dm7 G Dm7 G Dm7 Dm7add4
Keep me alone.

Verse 2

C   Dm7
Davy,

F Gsus4 G   F
   Are you the heat

      Am   Bb   G
I feel ___ in my foolish heart?

C   Dm7
Davy,

F Gsus4   G   Dm7 C/E
   There's not ___ a day

F   Am   Bb
   That I haven't prayed

D/F#   Dm/F   Am7   Dm7*
   To feel something so worthy,

    D+   G
For someone like you.

Interlude

$\frac{4}{4}$ Dm7 G Dm7 G	$\frac{2}{4}$ Dm7	$\frac{4}{4}$		Am G/B	
C Dm7 C/E F	Am G	Fmaj7 Gsus4	Am G/B	
C Dm7 C/E F	Am G	F G/F F		G	

Verse 3

```
C   Dm7
Davy,

F  Gsus4     G      F          Am
  Could there be love ____ so bright,

      Bb              G
Like to jump off the sea?

     C   Dm7  F
Da     -      vy,

Gsus4 G  Dm7 C/E     F
Did I   imag   -   ine it,

          Am     Bb
Or did you look at me

D/F#  Dm/F          Am7
        With a look so bold

Dm7*   D+          G
  That I had to look away?

      Dm7   G      Dm7   G
But if it feels all right, if it feels all right,

   Dm7   G       Dm7   G
If it feels all right, if it feels all right,

     Dm7   G      Dm7   G
If it feels all right, if it feels all right,

       Dm7   Dm7add4
And it feels all right,

C  Dm7  F
Davy,

Gsus4  G  C  Dm7  F  Gsus4  G  C
       Oh, Davy.
```

Do the Walls Come Down

Words and Music by
Carly Simon and Paul Samwell-Smith

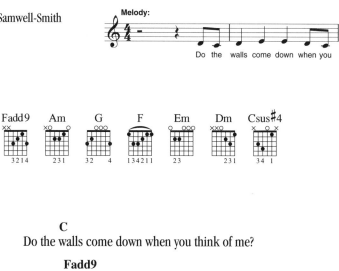

Chorus 1

         C
Do the walls come down when you think of me?

         Fadd9
Do your eyes grow dim?

         C
Do the walls come down when you think of me?

         Fadd9
Do you let me in?

         C
Do the walls come down?

Verse 1

         Am
Nothing like a rainy night

         G
To set your heart remembering.

F
Nothing like a vivid dream

         C
Take you back again.

Chorus 2

            C   Fadd9
When you think of me do your eyes grow dim?

            C
Do the walls come down when you think of me?

          Fadd9   C
Do you let me in? Do the walls come down?

Verse 2

          Am
   Something in my pocket

            Em
That was written years ago

         Dm
In faded ink said, "You are my fire."

           C
Do you think so?

Tin Whistle Solo

‖: C | | G | |

| F | | C | Csus#4 :‖

Chorus 3

Repeat Chorus 1

Verse 3

          Am
Is it easier for you to say

           G
You never loved me anyway.

          F
Or do you hide me in your attic trunk

           C
Like a stowaway?

	C Fadd9
Chorus 4	Do you think of me? Do your eyes grow dim?

C
Do the walls come down when you think of me?

Fadd9
Do you let me in?

C
  Oh, baby, do the walls come down?

Fadd9
  Oh, baby, do the walls come down?

C
‖:   Do the walls come, do the walls come,

Fadd9
  Do the walls come down? :‖ *Play 3 times*

     C
When you think of me.

Outro | Am | | Em | |

                  | Dm | | N.C. | ‖

Give Me All Night

Words and Music by
Carly Simon and Gerard McMahon

Melody:

I have no need __ of half __ of an-y-thing, __

| Cadd9 | Am7 | G | Fadd9 | C | Fmaj7 | Gadd9 | Gsus4 |

| E+ | C/D | C/E | F | F/G | F6 | Fmaj9 | Dm7 |

| Dm7* | F/C | Bbsus2 | Dm9 | Bb | F/A | G13 | G9 |

Intro

| Cadd9 | | | Am7 | |
| | G   Fadd9 | | | |

Verse 1

    C   Am7
  I have no need of half ____ of anything,

  Fmaj7   **Gadd9**
No half time, no half a man's attention.

  C   Am7
  Give me all the earth ____ and sky

    Fmaj7   **Gsus4**
And at the same time add a new dimension.

Fmaj7   **E+**
  Half the truth is of no ____ use.

     Am7
Give it all, ____ give it all to me.

     C/D
I can stand ____ it.

     C/E   **F F/G**
I am strong ____ that way.

Chorus 1

        C
Give me all night.

            Am7
Give me the full moon.

             Fmaj7 F6
And if I can't take the whole of you,

Fmaj7 F6   Gsus4
        Give it to me anyway.

            C   Am7
Give me all night till the last star fades.

             Fmaj7 F6
And if you can't take my heart and soul,

Fmaj7 F6   Gsus4 Fmaj9 Dm7
        Take it from me anyway.

Verse 2

C   Am7
  Don't give me fountains, I need waterfalls.

             Fmaj7 Gadd9
And when I cry my tears'll fill an ocean.

C   Am7
  The pain of love, I'll accept ___ it all

             Fmaj7   Gsus4
As long as you'll join me in that emotion.

Fmaj7   E+
  'Cause half of lovin' is no ___ fun.

            Am7
Give it all, ___ give it all to me.

            C/D
I can stand ___ it.

            C/E   F F/G
I am strong ___ that way.

Chorus 2

        C
Give me all night.

       Am7
Give me the full moon.

       Fmaj7 F6
And if I can't take the whole of you,

Fmaj7 F6   **Gsus4**
    Give it to me anyway.

       C   **Am7**
Give me all night till the last star fades.

         Fmaj7 F6
And if you can't take my heart and soul,

Fmaj7 F6   **Gsus4**
    Take it from me anyway.

Bridge

   Fmaj7 C/E   **Dm7* F/C B♭sus2**
Take all my breath away.

Fmaj7   **Dm9**
  Don't leave me guessing alone.

B♭   **F/A**   **F/G**
  Don't walk me half the way home.

G13   **F/G**
  You can do that tomor - row.

Outro-Chorus

G9 N.C.   **C**
  Just give me, give me all night.

      Am7
‖: Give me the full moon.

       Fmaj7 F6
And if I can't take the whole of you,

Fmaj7 F6   **Gsus4**
    Give it to me anyway.

       C   **Am7**
Give me all night till the last star fades.

        Fmaj7 F6
And if you can't take my heart and soul,

Fmaj7 F6   **Gsus4**
    Take it from me anyway.

C
Yeah, yeah, yeah. :‖ *Repeat and fade w/ vocal ad lib.*

Haven't Got Time for the Pain

Words and Music by
Carly Simon and Jacob Brackman

Melody:

All those _ cra - zy nights when I cried

Bm7   D/A   Gmaj7   Cadd9   Gadd2   G7   Am7   D

F   G   C   Em   F/G   G7*   D7

Verse 1

      Bm7   D/A
All those cra - zy nights

        Gmaj7   Cadd9
When I cried myself to sleep,

  Gmaj7   Cadd9   Gadd2 G7
   Now melodrama never makes me weep any - more.

Chorus 1

      Am7   D
'Cause I haven't got time for the pain,

    Am7   D
I haven't got room for the pain,

   F   Am7   D
I haven't the need for the pain,

 G   G7
  Not since I've known ____ you.

Verse 2

   C   D
  You showed me how,

     Em   Bm7
How to leave myself be - hind,

 Am7   D   Gadd2
How to turn down the noise ___ in my ___ mind.

Chorus 2

G7   Am7   D
   Now I haven't got time for the pain,

 Am7   D
I haven't got room for the pain,

 F   Am7   D
I haven't the need for the pain,

 G   F/G   G7* F/G G7*
 Not since I've ___ known you.

 Am7   D
I haven't got time for the pain,

 Am7   D
I haven't got room for the pain,

 F   Am7   D
I haven't the need for the pain.

Verse 3

Bm7   D/A
  Suffering was the only thing

         Gmaj7   Cadd9
Made me feel I was alive,

Gmaj7   Cadd9
Thought that's just how much it cost

       Gadd2   G7
To sur - vive in this world.

   C   D
Till you showed me how,

     Em   Bm7
How to fill my heart with love,

    Am7   D7   G
How to open up and drink ___ in all that white ___ light

        G7
Pouring down ___ from the heaven.

Chorus 3

Am7   **D**
Haven't got time for the pain,

Am7   **D**
I haven't got room for the pain,

F   **Am7**   **D**
I haven't the need for the pain,

G   **F/G**   **G7***   **F/G**   **G7***
   Not since I've ___ known you.

Outro-Chorus

   Am7   **D**
‖: I haven't got time for the pain.

Am7   **D**
I haven't got room for the pain.

Am7   **D**
I haven't the need for the pain.   :‖   ***Repeat and fade***
                                                 w/ vocal ad lib.

Happy Birthday

Words and Music by
Carly Simon

Melody:

It's all of our birth - days this ___ sum-mer.

Tune down 1/2 step:
(low to high) E♭-A♭-D♭-G♭-B♭-E♭

Am/D   G6(no3rd)   C   Am7   D   Em

Gm7   Dm   Dsus2   F   A7

Intro

| Am/D | | | G6(no3rd) | | |

Verse 1

       Am/D   G6(no 3rd)
It's all of our birthdays this summer.

   Am/D   G6(no3rd)
One number older, anoth - er year younger.

C   Am7   D   Em
I'll go to your ___ party, you'll come to mine.

    Gm7   C   Dm Dsus2 Dm
We've given up cigarettes, we've given up wine.

Verse 2

       Am/D   G6(no 3rd)
We've given up caffeine and sworn off desserts.

     Am/D   G6(no 3rd)
I don't try to seduce you, we don't even flirt.

           C   Am7   D   Em
We're too good ___ to be hap - py, too straight to be sad.

    Gm7   C
So just blow out the can - dles,

       Am/D G6(no 3rd) Am/D G6(no 3rd)
Happy Birth - day.

Verse 3

       Am/D   G6(no 3rd)
Stay out of the ocean, stay out of the sun.

       Am/D   G6(no 3rd)
Stay in perfect shape and be ___ number one.

         C   Am7   D   Em
We've got brilliant ex - cuses for having no fun,

      Gm7   C
So just blow out the can - dles,

         Am/D   G6(no 3rd) Am/D G6(no 3rd)
Happy Birth - day.

Bridge

Am7   D
Make love in the mic - rowave,

Am7   D
Think of all the time ___ you'll save.

    Am7   D
And don't forget to make ___ it look

    F   Gm7   A7
As though you're working very, very hard.

Interlude

‖: Am/D | |G6(no3rd) | :‖
Ooh, _____ ooh.

Verse 3

Am/D   G6(no 3rd)
I'll be your lover if you will be mine.

       Am/D   G6(no 3rd)
We'll go back ___ to the garden, and have ___ a good time.

       C   Am7   D   Em
If I'm offered an ap - ple, I'll po - litely decline, ___ ooh.

      Gm7   C
And just blow out the can - dles,

         Am/D   G6(no 3rd) Am/D G6(no 3rd)
Happy Birth - day.

Outro

         Am/D   G6(no 3rd)
‖: Happy Birth - day, Happy Birth - day. :‖ *Repeat and fade*
                                                   w/ vocal ad lib.

Jesse

Words and Music by
Carly Simon and Mike Mainieri

Melody:

Oh,   moth-er say a pray'r for me,

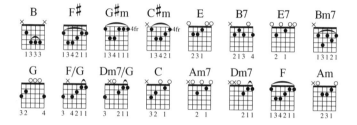

Verse 1

  B   F#   B
Oh, mother say a pray'r for me,

    F# B   F# B
Jesse's back in town, it won't be eas - y.

G#m   C#m
 Don't let him near me,

       E   F# B
Don't let him touch me, don't let him please me.

Chorus 1

  B G#m   E
Jesse, I won't cut fresh flow - ers for you.

   B G#m   E
No, Jesse, I won't make the wine cold ____ for you.

   B G#m   E
No Jesse, I won't change the sheets ____ for you.

    G#m   C#m   F#
I won't put on cologne, I won't sit by the phone for you.

Verse 2

B   F♯   B
Annie, keep re - minding me

      F♯   B   F♯   B
That he cut out my heart like a paper doll.

G♯m   C♯m
Sally, tell me once again

       E   F♯   B
How he set me up just to see me fall.

Chorus 2

B   G♯m   E
Jesse, I won't cut fresh flow - ers for you.

    B   G♯m   E
No, Jesse, I won't make the wine cold for you.

    B   G♯m   E
No, Jesse, I won't change the sheets ___ for you.

    G♯m   C♯m   F♯
I won't put on cologne, I won't sit by the phone for you.

            Bm7
No, no, no, no. Jesse!

Bridge

N.C.(Bm7)   E7
Quick! Come here, I won't tell a soul, *not even myself.*

Bm7
Jesse, that you've come back to me,

  E7
My friends will all say, *"She's gone again."*

  G
But how can anyone know what you are to me?

    F/G   Dm7/G
That I'm in heaven again, because you've come back to me.

Guitar Solo

| C | G C | G C | G C |
| Am7 | Dm7 | F | G C |

Chorus 3

C Am   F
Jesse, I'll always cut fresh flow - ers for you.

  C   Am   F
And Jesse, I'll always make the wine cold ___ for you.

  C   Am   F
Oh Jesse, I can easily change my mind ___ about you,

  Am   Dm7   G
And put on cologne, and sit ___ by the phone for you.

Verse 3

     C   G   C
Oh yeah, ___ Jesse, let's open the wine

 G   C   G   C
And drink to the heart which has a will of its own.

  Am   Dm7
My friends, let's comfort them.

     F   G   C
They're feeling bad, they think I've sunk so low.

Chorus 4

C Am   F
Jesse, I'll always cut fresh flow - ers for you.

  C Am   F
And Jesse, I will make the wine cold ___ for you.

   C   Am   F
Oh ___ Jesse, I will change the sheets ___ for you.

Am   Dm7   G
Put on cologne, and I will wait by the phone for you.

Verse 4

   C   G   C
Oh, Jessie!
  (La, la, la, la, la, la, la,

    G   C   G   C
La, la, la, la, la, la, la, la, la, la.)

    Am   Dm7
Oh, Jessie!
  (La, la, la, la, la, la, la,

    F   G   C
La, la, la, la, la, la, la, la, la, la.)

Outro-Chorus   *Repeat Chorus 4 and fade*

Legend in Your Own Time

Words and Music by
Carly Simon

Melody:

Well, I have known _ you

E7	Am7	Dm7	Amaj7	D9	E	F#m7	Em7	E7*
3 2 4 1	1 3 1 1 1 1	1 3 1 2 1	2 3 1	2 1 3 3 3	2 3 1	1 3 1 1 1 1	1 2 4	2 3 1 4

Verse 1

      E7   **Am7**
Well, I have known ____ you

Dm7   **Am7**
Since you were a small ____ boy,

Dm7   **Am7**   **Dm7**
And your ma - ma used to say,

              Am7
"Well, my boy ____ is gonna grow up

         Dm7   **Am7**
And be ____ some kind of leader some - day."

Pre-Chorus 1

     Dm7   **E7**
Then you'd turn on the radio

       Amaj7
And sing with the singer in the band.

   Am7
Your mama would say to you,

      D9   **E7**
"This isn't exactly what we had planned."

Chorus 1

         Am7   **Dm7**
But you're a legend in your own ____ time,

  Am7   **Dm7**
I hero in the foot - lights,

Am7   **Dm7**
   Playing tunes to fit ____ your rhyme,

       D9   **E7**
But a leg - end's only a lone - ly boy

       Am7   **Dm7**
When he ____ goes home alone.

Interlude

| Am7 | Dm7 | E F#m7 Em7 | E7* | |

Verse 2

          Am7
And though I ____ know you

Dm7   **Am7**
   Still have the heart of that small ____ boy.

Dm7   **Am7**   **Dm7**
   Well, you lend ____ it out far too much,

     Am7   **Dm7**
And no ____ one woman loving you can ever feel

       Am7
That she's been really touched.

	Dm7 **E7**
Pre-Chorus 2	Then you turn on the radio

Dm7   **E7**

Pre-Chorus 2

Then you turn on the radio

   Amaj7

And sing with the singer in the band.

Am7

You think kind of sadly to yourself,

   D9   **E7**

"This isn't exactly what you had planned."

         Am7   **Dm7**

Chorus 2

But you're a legend in your own ___ time,

   Am7   **Dm7**

I hero in the foot - lights,

Am7   **Dm7**

Playing tunes to fit ___ your rhyme,

     D9   **E7**

But a leg - end's only a lone - ly boy

      Am7   **Dm7 Am7**

When he ___ goes home alone.

Dm7   **D9**   **E7**

Well, a leg - end's only a lone - ly boy

      Am7   **Dm7**

When he ___ goes home alone.

Outro   ‖: **Am7** | **Dm7**   :‖ *Repeat and fade*

Let the River Run
Theme from the Motion Picture
WORKING GIRL

Words and Music by
Carly Simon

Melody:

Let the riv-er run,

Chord diagrams: E A C#m B A/E F#/A# E/G#
D B/A B/G# B/F# F# F#sus4 Eadd2

Intro   ‖: E | A   :‖

Verse 1
       E   A
Let the river run,
            E   C#m B
Let all the dreamers wake the na - tion.
A   C#m B   E   A/E E A/E
Come, the new Je - ru - sa - lem.

Verse 2
       E   A
Silver cities rise,
            E   C#m B
The morning lights the streets that lead   them,
       A   C#m B   E   A/E E
And sirens call them on   with a song.

Bridge 1
       C#m   F#/A#
It's asking for the taking,
A   E/G#
Trembling, shaking.
C#m   D
Oh, my heart is aching.
       B   B/A
We're coming to the edge, running on the water,
B/G#   B/F#   B
Coming through the fog, your sons and daughters.

Verse 3

```
        E              A
We, the great and small,

              E              C♯m B      A
Stand on a star and blaze a trail   of de - sire

              C♯m   B    E    A/E  E
Through the dark - 'ning dawn.
```

Bridge 2

```
              C♯m          F♯/A♯
It's asking for the taking.

        A                                      E/G♯
Come run with me now, the sky is the color of blue

                                    C♯m
You've never even seen in the eyes of your lover.

                    D
Oh, my heart is aching.

            B                  B/A
We're coming to the edge, running on the water,

B/G♯                        B/F♯      B
Coming through the fog, your sons and daughters.
```

Outro

```
        E        A
Let the river run,

              E              C♯m B
Let all the dreamers wake the na  -  tion.

A              C♯m B  F♯
Come, the new Je - ru  - sa - lem.

C♯m                B  F♯ F♯sus4 F♯
Come the new Jeru - sa - lem.

C♯m              B  Eadd2
Come the new Jeru - sa - lem.
```

Libby

Words and Music by
Carly Simon

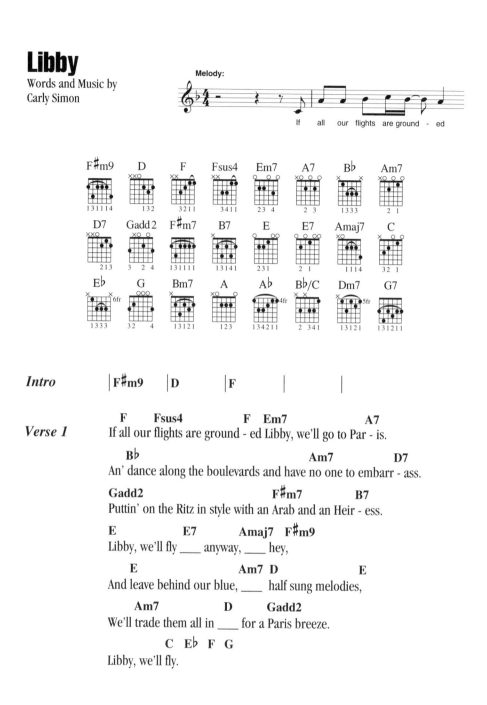

Melody:

If all our flights are ground - ed

F#m9 D F Fsus4 Em7 A7 Bb Am7

D7 Gadd2 F#m7 B7 E E7 Amaj7 C

Eb G Bm7 A Ab Bb/C Dm7 G7

Intro | F#m9 | D | F | | |

Verse 1

       F   **Fsus4**   **F** **Em7**   **A7**
If all our flights are ground - ed Libby, we'll go to Par - is.

    Bb   **Am7**   **D7**
An' dance along the boulevards and have no one to embarr - ass.

Gadd2   **F#m7**   **B7**
Puttin' on the Ritz in style with an Arab and an Heir - ess.

E   **E7**   **Amaj7** **F#m9**
Libby, we'll fly ____ anyway, ____ hey,

     E   **Am7** **D**   **E**
And leave behind our blue, ____ half sung melodies,

   Am7   **D**   **Gadd2**
We'll trade them all in ____ for a Paris breeze.

        C **Eb** **F** **G**
Libby, we'll fly.

Verse 2

C   Bm7   E7
See how dark the circles grow in a town ___ that has no light.

 A   F#m7   B7
So many eyes just staring out in - to the bloodshot night.

 E   E7   Amaj7
And Libby, I hate ___ to see you cry,

 F#m9 E   Am7
And I wanna share it all with you,

   D   E
And if it brings us to our knees,

  Am7   D   Gadd2
We'll trade it all in ___ for a Paris breeze.

     C Eb Ab Bb/C
Libby, we'll fly.

Verse 3

   F   Em7   A7
They say it don't come easy and they say ___ that love is blind.

 Bb   Am7   D7
If you're afraid to be close then love ___ is hard to find.

   G
And if you spend too much time winning love

  F#m7   B7
There's no time to be kind.

  E   E7   Amaj7
And Libby, I'm guilty of your crimes,

F#m9   E   Am7
I'm just an - other passenger

D   E
Trav'lin' on these crazy high seas,

Am7   D   Gadd2
Very likely be the same in a Paris breeze.

     C Eb Ab Bb/C
Libby, we'll fly _____ away.

| *Instrumental* | |F |Em7 A7 |B♭ |Am7 D7 | |

Verse 4

     E♭   Dm7   G7
If all our flights are grounded, Libby, we'll go to Pa - ris

       C   Bm7   E7
And wish we were back home again or sailing on the o - cean.

       A   F#m7   B7
Just a window and a drink to set our dreams ___ in mo - tion.

   E   E7   Amaj7 F#m9
But Libby, we'll fly ___ anyway, ____ hey,

   E   Am7 D   E
And leave our blue, half-sung melodies,

Am7   D7   Gadd2
Trade them in for a Paris breeze.

          C E♭ F G
Libby, we'll fly.

Love of My Life

from the Motion Picture
THIS IS MY LIFE

Words and Music by
Carly Simon

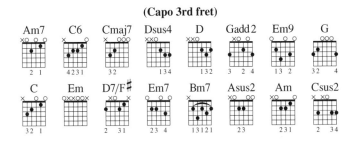

Melody:

I love _ li - lacs _

(Capo 3rd fret)

Am7   C6   Cmaj7   Dsus4   D   Gadd2   Em9   G

C   Em   D7/F#   Em7   Bm7   Asus2   Am   Csus2

Intro |Am7 | |

Verse 1
    C6 Cmaj7 Dsus4 D
I   love   li - lacs

    C6 Cmaj7 Gadd2
And av - ocados,

C6   Cmaj7   Dsus4 D
Uku - leles and fire - works

    Em9   G   C
And Mia Farrow and walking in the snow.

        D Em D7/F#
But you've got to know…

Chorus 1

       G   **Em7**
That you're the love of my life,

       D   **Bm7**   **Am7**
You are the love of my life.

G   **Em7**
You are the love of my life,

       D   **Am7**
You are the love of my life.

        Bm7   **Em9**
From the moment I first saw ___ you,

      Am7   **C**   **D**
The second that you were born,

           G   **Em7**
I knew that you were the love of my life,

      D   **Am7**   **Bm7** **C** **D** **G** **Gadd2** **G**
Quite simply   the love ___ of my life.

Verse 2

C6 **Cmaj7** **Dsus4** **D**
I   love   Lu - cy

      C6   **Cmaj7**   **Gadd2**
And pumper - nickel bread,

      C6   **Cmaj7** **Dsus4** **D**
The Stat - ue of   Liber - ty

      Em9   **G**   **C**
And chocolate ice cream and falling into bed.

                   D **Em** **D7/F♯**
You get it through your head...

Chorus 2

        G   **Em7**
That you're the love of my life,

    D   **Bm7**   **Am7**
You are the love of my life.

G   **Em7**   **D**
You are the love of my ___ life,

       Am7
You are the love of my life.

     Bm7   **Em9**
From the moment I first saw ___ you,

   Am7   **C D**
The second that you were born,

        G   **Em7**
I knew that you were the love of my life,

    D   **Am7 Bm7** C **D G Gadd2 G**
Quite simply the love _____ of my life.

       Asus2 Am   **Bm7 Csus2 Am7**   **Gadd2**
You are the love,   the great love of my,   of my life.

Like a River

Words and Music by
Carly Simon

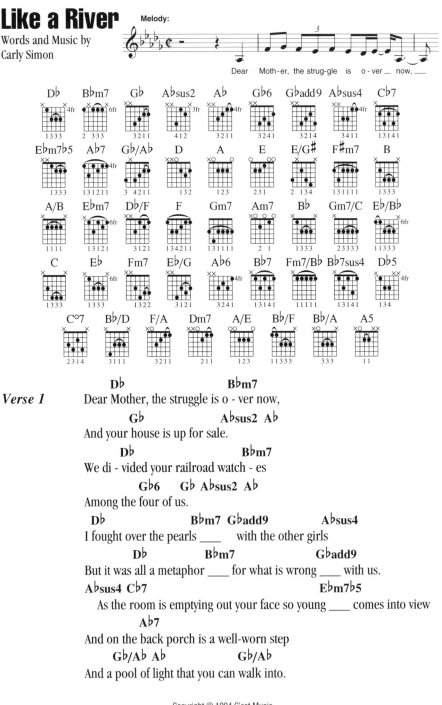

Verse 1

         Db   Bbm7
Dear Mother, the struggle is o - ver now,

          Gb   Absus2 Ab
And your house is up for sale.

         Db   Bbm7
We di - vided your railroad watch - es

          Gb6   Gb Absus2 Ab
Among the four of us.

        Db   Bbm7 Gbadd9   Absus4
I fought over the pearls ____ with the other girls

           Db   Bbm7   Gbadd9
But it was all a metaphor ____ for what is wrong ____ with us.

Absus4 Cb7   Ebm7b5
   As the room is emptying out your face so young ____ comes into view

        Ab7
And on the back porch is a well-worn step

       Gb/Ab Ab   Gb/Ab
And a pool of light that you can walk into.

Chorus 1

```
        D         A          E
```
I'll wait no more for you   like a daughter.

```
        D                A          E     E/G♯
```
That part of our life ___ together is o - ver,

```
        F♯m7      E      A      E       B    A/B  B
```
But I will wait for you   forev - er, ___ like a river.

Verse 2

```
| D♭      | B♭m7     | G♭add9  | A♭sus4   |
```

```
        D♭                B♭m7
```
Can you clear up the mystery of ___ the Sphinx?

```
        G♭add9          A♭sus4
```
Do you know any more about God?

```
        D♭                    B♭m7
```
Are you dancing with Benjamin Frank - lin

```
        G♭add9          A♭sus4
```
On the face ___ of the moon?

```
        D♭                B♭m7
```
Have you reconciled with Dad?

```
        G♭add9                A♭sus4
```
Does the rain ___ still make you sad?

```
    D♭                  B♭m7                    G♭add9
```
Last night, I swear I could feel ___ you moving through ___ my room.

```
A♭sus4 C♭7                       E♭m7♭5
```
     I thought you touched my feet, I so want - ed it to be true.

```
        A♭7
```
And in my ___ theater there is a stage

```
        G♭/A♭  A♭         G♭/A♭
```
And a footlight you can always step into.

Chorus 2

```
        D      A          E
```
I'll wait no more for you ___ like a daughter.

```
        D                A          E     E/G♯
```
That part of our life ___ together is o - ver,

```
        F♯m7      E      A E       B
```
But I will wait for you ___ forev - er, like a river.
```
```

Instrumental	E		F#m7		
	E/G#		A		A/B	

Verse 3

| Db | Bbm7 | Gbadd9 | Absus4 |

       Db   Bbm7
In the river I know I will find ____ the key

                Gbadd9   Absus4
And your voice ____ will rise like spray.

          Db   Bbm7   Gbadd9
In the moment of knowing, the tide ____ will wash a - way my doubt.

Absus4 Db   Bbm7
   'Cause you're already home

        Gbadd9
Makin' it nice for when I come,

        Db   Bbm7
Like the way I find my bed ____ turned down

        Gbadd9   Absus4
Coming in ____ from a late-night out.

        Cb7   Ebm7b5
Please keep reminding me of what in my soul ____ I know is true.

               Ab7
Come in my boat, ____ there is a seat beside me

     Gb/Ab   Ab   Gb/Ab
And two or three stars that we can gaze into.

Chorus 3

        D   A   E
I'll wait no more for you ____ like a daughter.

        D   A   E   E/G#
That part of our life ____ together is o - ver,

        F#m7   E
But I will wait for you

      A E   B
Forev - er, like a river.

Postlude

          D♭   **E♭m7**
I'll never leave, always just a dream away,

          D♭/F Gb6
A star that's always watching,

E♭m7   **A♭**
Never turn a - way.

    Gb/A♭ F   **Gm7**
We'll never   leave, always just a thought away,

  Am7 B♭   **Gm7/C E♭/B♭**   **C**
A candle always burning, never turn a - way.

         E♭   **Fm7**
The moon will hide, the dance will end,

     E♭/G   **Ab6 B♭7 Fm7/B♭ B♭7sus4 B♭7**
But in the wind the tree _____ will   bend.

D♭5   **C°7 B♭/D**
  I'm right be - side you.

B♭ **F/A Dm7**
  I'll never turn,

  A/E B♭/F B♭/A A5
I'll never turn   a - way.

Lost in Your Love

Words and Music by
Carly Simon

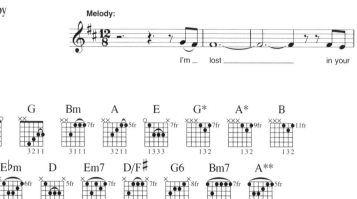

Chorus 1

      F#7   G
I'm lost in your love,

      F#7   G
So lost in my love for you.

       Bm   A
Ev'ry - thing that you say,

       G   F#7
Ev'ry - thing that you do.

      E   G* A*   B
I'm lost ___ in your love.

Verse 1

        Ebm   D
I can find me a night so lovely it might even change me.

       Bm
I can't find me a place where mornings come from,

      Em7 D/F#   G6   Bm7 A** N.C.
But I'm lost   when it comes to   you.

Chorus 2

    F#7   G
So lost in your love,

    F#7   G
So lost in my love for you.

      Bm   A
And I can't see your face

          G   F#7
'Cause I'm tumbling through space

     E   G* A*   B
I'm lost ____ in your love.

Verse 2

    E♭m   D
Find me, take me, hold me.

    Bm
I can't let you go free

       Em7 D/F# G6 Bm7 A** N.C.
Till you lose   your - self in   me,   oh.

Sax Solo

F#7		G		
F#7		G	Bm A	
3/8 G	12/8 F#7	E G*	A* N.C.	

Outro-Chorus

    F#7   G
I'm ____ lost, so lost in ____ your love,

    F#7   G
So lost in my love for you.

      Bm   A
Ev'ry - thing that you say,

      G   F#7
Ev'ry - thing that you do.

     E   G* A*   B
I'm ____ lost ____ in your love.

     E   G* A*   B
I'm lost ____   in your love.

E   G*   A* B
  (So lost, so lost.   so lost,   lost in your love.)

    E   G* A*   B
So lost ____ in your love.

Never Been Gone

Words and Music by
Carly Simon and Jacob Brackman

Melody:

Ooh,   ooh,   ooh, ooh, ooh,   ooh,

Chords: B, F#, D#m, E, C#m, F#m, Gb, Ab, Fm, Bbm, Ebm, Db, Db7, F7sus4, F7, Eb, Fm7, Ebm7

Intro

   B   F#   B
Ooh, ooh, ooh, ooh, ooh,
    D#m   E   F#
Ooh, ooh, ooh, ooh, ooh, ooh,
        B   F#
Ooh, ooh, ooh, ooh, ooh, ooh, ooh, ooh, ooh, ooh,
     C#m   F#
Ooh, ooh, ooh, ooh, ooh, ooh, ooh, ooh, ooh.
    B   F#m B
Ah, ah, ah, ah, ah, ah,
    D#m E   F#
Ah, ah, ah, ah, ah, ah,
       B   F#
Ah, ah, ah, ah, ah, ah, ah, ah, ah, ah,
    C#m   F#
Ah, ah, ah, ah, ah, ah, ah, ah, ah,
    B
Ah, ah, ah.

Verse 1

Gb   Ab   Fm   Bbm
   The wind is coming up strong and fast
       Ebm Ab   Db Db7
And the moon is smiling on me.
Gb   Ab   Fm   Bbm
Miles from no - where so small at last
     Gb   Ab   F7sus4 F7
In be - tween the sky ___ and the sea.

GUITAR CHORD SONGBOOK

Chorus 1

    Db   Eb   Fm Gb
I'm bound for the island the tide is with me,

   Db   Fm   Gb
I think I can make ____ it by dawn.

    Db   Eb   Fm Gb
It's night on the ocean and I'm going home,

And it feels like I've never,

     Fm7 Ebm7 Db
I've nev - er   been   gone.

Verse 2

Gb   Ab   Fm   Bbm
Seagulls cry and the hills are green

    Ebm   Ab   Db Db7
And my friends are waiting for me.

Gb   Ab   Fm   Bbm
Great am - bition is all a dream.

    Ebm   Ab   F7sus4 F7
Let me drown my pride ____ in the sea.

Chorus 2

    Db   Eb   Fm Gb
I'm bound for the island the tide is with me,

   Db   Fm   Gb
I think I can make ____ it by dawn.

    Db   Eb   Fm Gb
Oh, it's night on the ocean and I'm going home,

And it feels like I've never,

     Fm7 Ebm7 Db
I've nev - er   been   gone.

    Gb
Oh, it feels like I've never,

     Fm7 Ebm7 Db Cb Gb Db
I've nev - er   been   gone.   Hmm.

Nobody Does It Better

from THE SPY WHO LOVED ME

Music by Marvin Hamlisch
Lyrics by Carole Bayer Sager

Melody:

No - bod-y does   it   bet - ter,

F F°7 E°7 F6 E6 E♭6 F7 B♭ B♭m

B♭m6 A7#5♭9 A7♭9 Dm7 Gm7 B♭/C F/A G9 G♭9

F7/A A7 D7#9 C7 B♭maj7 Bm7♭5 D♭ E♭ E

Intro | F   F°7 E°7 | F   F6   E6   E♭6   F7 |

Chorus 1
      B♭   B♭m   F   F7
      Nobody does ____ it bet - ter,
      B♭   B♭m   F   F7
      Makes me feel sad ____ for ____ the rest.
      B♭   B♭m6 A7#5♭9 A7♭9 Dm7
      Nobody does ____ it   half   as   good as you.
      Gm7 B♭/C   F   F°7 E°7
      Ba - by, you're the best.

Verse 1
      F   F/A
      I wasn't look - in',
      B♭   B♭m
      But somehow you found ____ me.
      F   F/A   G9 G♭9
      I tried to hide ____ from your love light,
      F   F7/A
      But, like heaven above ____ me,
      B♭   B♭m
      The spy who loved ____ me
      A7   D7#9 Gm7   C7   F   F7
      Is keepin' all my secrets safe ____ to - night.

Chorus 2

      B♭   B♭m   F   F7
And   nobody does ___ it bet - ter,

      B♭   B♭m   F   F7
Though sometimes I wish some - one could.

      B♭   B♭m6 A7#5♭9 A7♭9 Dm7
Nobody does ___ it   quite the way ___ you do.

      Gm7   B♭/C   F   F°7 E°7
Why'd you have to be so good?

Verse 2

      F   F/A
The way that you hold ___ me

      B♭   B♭m
Whenever you hold ___ me,

      F   F7/A   G9 G♭9
There's some kind of mag - ic in - side ___ you,

      F   F/A
That keeps me from run - nin',

      B♭   B♭m
But just keep it com - in'.

      A7   D7#9   Gm7   C7   F   F7
How'd you learn ___ to do ___ the things ___ you ___ do?

Chorus 3

           B♭   B♭m   F   F7
Oh, and   nobody does ___ it bet - ter,

      B♭   B♭m   F   F7
Makes me feel sad ___ for ___ the rest.

      B♭   B♭m6 A7#5♭9 A7♭9 Dm7
Nobody does ___ it   half   as   good as you.

      Gm7   F/A   B♭maj7 Bm7♭5
Baby, ___ baby,   dar - lin'

      B♭/C   F   F/A B♭
You're the best.

       D♭   E♭   E   F   F/A B♭
‖: Baby, you're the best.   :‖ *Play 7 times w/ vocal ad lib.*
      D♭   E♭   E F   F°7 E°7 F F7
Baby, you're the best.

Older Sister

Words and Music by
Carly Simon

Melody:

She rides in the front seat,

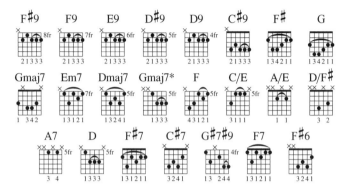

Intro |F#9 F9 |E9 D#9 |D9   C#9| |

Verse 1

       F#
She rides in the front seat, she's my older sister.

   G   **F#**
   She knows her power over me.

Gmaj7   **Em7**   **Dmaj7**
   She goes to bed an hour later than I do.

                      Gmaj7*
When she turns the lights out

   Dmaj7   **Gmaj7***
What does she think about?

       F   **C/E**
And what does she do in the daylight

      A/E **D/F#**   **A7**
That makes her so great?

Chorus 1

D   F#7
Oh, but to be, oh, but to be,

D   F#7   D   C#7
Oh, but to be, I'd like to be my older ___ sister.

Verse 2

     F#
She flies ___ through the back door, she's my older sister.

G   F#
 She throws French phrases 'round the room.

Gmaj7   Em7   Dmaj7
 She has ice skates and legs that fit ___ right in.

           Gmaj7* Dmaj7
She's wicked to all the beaming dreamers

   Gmaj7* F   C/E
Who lat - er boast of an evening

     A/E D/F# A7
By her fier - y side.

Chorus 2

D   F#7
Oh, but to be, I'd ___ like to be,

D   F#7   D C#7
Please let me be, oh, let me be my older sister.

Bridge

    D#9
And in her black gymnastic tights she runs into some elastic nights.

    G#7#9
So - phisticated sister sings for the soldiers of the soccer team.

   F7
Their silver I.D.'s and sororities, they tinker with love in their Model T's.

   C#7   F#
Oh Lord, won't you let me be her for just ___ one day.

Verse 3

F♯   G
(Ba, ba, ba, ba, ooh,

F♯
Older sister, my older sister.

Gmaj7   Em7   Dmaj7
Whoa, it to be older sister.)

                       Gmaj7*
She turns ev'rybody's heads

            Dmaj7   Gmaj7*
While I wear her last year's threads

      F   C/E
With patches and stitches

       A/E   D/F♯ A7
And a turned up   hem.

Chorus 3

D   F♯7
Oh, but to be, oh, but to be,

D   F♯7   D   F♯6 F♯7
I'd like to be, just once to be my old - er sister.

Outro | F♯9 F9 | E9 D♯9 | D9 C♯9 F♯6 | ‖

Our Affair

Words and Music by
Carly Simon

Melody:

What a per-fect night, — se-crets light up the sky —

Chord diagrams: Bm, A/B, A, D, Amaj7, Dsus2, Am, F, G, C, A*, E, C#m, F#

Prelude

    Bm   A/B   Bm
    What a perfect night,

    A/B   A   D
Secrets light up the sky ____ like fireflies do.

    Bm
There's nothing but a silky hope,

     Amaj7   D Dsus2 D Dsus2
That old opiate be - tween me and you.

Verse 1

Am F G
Don't look now

Am   F   G
 We're just ____ about there,

Am   F   C   G
 We're just one little breath a - way

Chorus 1

           Am D Am D
From our af - fair,

           Am D Am D
From our af - fair.

Verse 2

       Bm   **G**   **A***
Don't move ____ too fast,

       Bm   **G** **A***
Don't run ____ scared.

       Bm   **G**   **D**   **A**
We're just one sur - render a - way, away

Chorus 2

                  Bm E Bm E
From our af - fair,

                  Bm E Bm E
From our af - fair.

Bridge 1

       Bm   **E**   **Bm**   **E**
Don't ____ you feel like you're coming down with something,

A   **D**
Some great, fancy flu?

       Bm   **E**   **Bm**   **E**
Don't ____ you feel like you're coming down with me?

       C♯m   **D**
And it doesn't get sicker than ____ you.

Bridge 2

   Bm   **E**   **Bm**   **E**
Don't you feel like this is a really good part

          A   **D** **C♯m**
Where it's still up in the air?

     Bm   **E**   **Bm** **E**
The perfect romance is never stated

    C♯m   **D**
Or sated, deflated or fair.

Verse 3

Am   F   G
Don't ad - mit it yet,

Am   F   G
Don't stop saying your prayers.

Am   F   C   G
We're just one little heartbeat a - way

Chorus 3

          Am D Am D
From our af - fair,

          Am D Am D
From our af - fair.

Verse 4

       Bm   G   A*
There's a light in ____ my window

       Bm   G   A*
And a little red ladybug in my hair.

Bm   G   D   A
Just one turn down an empty street away, away, away

Outro-Chorus

         Bm E Bm E
‖: From our af - fair,

         Bm E Bm E
From our af - fair,

        C#m F# C#m F#
From our af - fair,

        C#m F# C#m F#
From our af - fair.   :‖ *Repeat and fade*

The Right Thing to Do

Words and Music by
Carly Simon

Melody:

There's noth-in' you can do to turn ___ me a - way, ___

Cadd9　Fmaj7　Dm9　F/G　Am7　F#m7　B　Em7

G/A　Dmaj7　Dm7　Dm7/G　G/C　Am9　Gm7　C

Cmaj9　C7　F　Bb　F/A　G6　Fmaj9　Cmaj13

Intro　　|N.C.　　|　　|

Verse 1

　　　　　　Cadd9　　　　　　　　Fmaj7
There's nothin' you can do to turn ___ me away,

Dm9　　　　F/G　　Am7
　Nothin' any - one can say.

　　F#m7　　　　　B　　　　Em7
You're with me now ___ and as long as you stay,

　G/A　　　　　　　　　Dmaj7
Lov - in' you's the right thing to do.

　Dm7　　　　　Fmaj7　Dm7/G
Lov - in' you's the right　　thing.

Verse 2

N.C.　Cadd9　　　　　　　　　　　　　　　Fmaj7
　Oh, I know you've had some bad luck with la - dies before,

　　Dm9　　　　　　F/G　　　　Am7
They drove you or you drove them cra - zy.

　　　　F#m7　　　　B　　　　　　　　Em7
But more impor - tant is I ___ know you're the one,

　　　　　　G/A　　　　　　　Dmaj7
And I'm sure lov - in' you's right thing to do,

　Dm7　　　　　Fmaj7　Dm7/G
Lov - in' you's the right　　thing.

GUITAR CHORD SONGBOOK

Bridge

N.C.   Dm7   G/C
Oh, and it used to be for a while

     Am9   Gm7   C
That the river flowed right to ___ my door,

Dm7   Cmaj9
Making me just a little too free.

       Am9
But now the river doesn't seem

       Gm7   C7   F B♭ F/A F/G G6
To stop ___ here anymore.

Verse 3

Cadd9   Fmaj7
Hold me in your hands like a bunch of flowers.

Dm9   F/G   Am7
  Set me movin' to your sweetest song.

  F♯m7   B   Em7
And I know what I ___ think I've known all along,

  G/A   Dmaj7
Lov - in' you's the right thing to do.

Dm7   Fmaj7 Dm7/G
Lovin' you's the right   thing.

Outro

Dm7/G   Cadd9
Lovin' you's the right thing to do,

Fmaj9   Cadd9
  Is the right thing to do.

Fmaj9   Cadd9
  Nothing you can ever do would turn me a - way from you.

  Fmaj9   Cadd9
I love ___ you now, and I love ___ you now.

  Fmaj9   Cadd9
E - ven though you're ten thousand miles ___ away.

  Fmaj9   Cadd9
I'll love ___ you tomorrow as I love ___ you today.

  Fmaj9 Cadd9   Fmaj9   Cadd9
I'm in love, babe. ___ I'm in love ___ with you, babe.

Fmaj9   Cadd9 Fmaj9   Cadd9
  The right thing to do, ___   the right thing to do.

Fmaj9   Cadd9   Fmaj9   Cmaj13
  The right thing to do. ___ Let's close ___ now.

So Many Stars

Words and Music by
Carly Simon

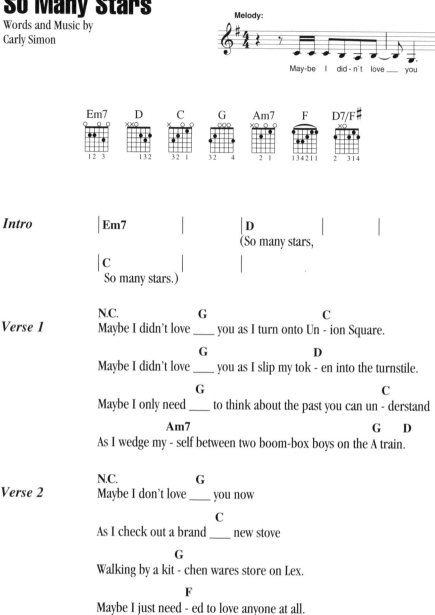

Intro

| Em7 | | | D | | |
(So many stars,

| C | | |
So many stars.)

Verse 1

    N.C.   G   C
Maybe I didn't love ____ you as I turn onto Un - ion Square.

                        G   D
Maybe I didn't love ____ you as I slip my tok - en into the turnstile.

                   G   C
Maybe I only need ____ to think about the past you can un - derstand

              Am7   G   D
As I wedge my - self between two boom-box boys on the A train.

Verse 2

    N.C.   G
Maybe I don't love ____ you now

                     C
As I check out a brand ____ new stove

              G
Walking by a kit - chen wares store on Lex.

              F
Maybe I just need - ed to love anyone at all.

Bridge

Em7
Maybe I won't ever love you again

D
As I walk ___ into Manny's for some strings.

C   D
Maybe we won't ever be friends.

Verse 3

G
Could I have needed ___ to love the dark

C
As I try to avoid ___ a jackey on Broome?

G   D
Could I have con - jured you on imag - inary avenues.

Verse 4

C   D
Well, maybe I need to merge ___ with the all

D7/F♯   G
As I stare at the sunset over the Hudson.

Em7   F   C
And there you'd become one of so ___ many stars.

Verse 5

C
What if I couldn't tell ___ you apart?

G
What if I couldn't pick ___ out your face?

F   C
What if I didn't love ___ you? Didn't love ___ you.

Instrumental | C | | G | |

Outro

Am7   F
   There are so many stars.

C   G
   What if I couldn't pick out your face,   or find your hands.

Am7   F   C
   There are so many stars.   What if I didn't love you?

G
   But what if I do? How will I know?

                                    Am7
What will you do when I find ___ you?

                F   C   G
There are so many stars.

Am7   F
   There are so ___ many stars.

C
   What if you're out there and I just didn't see you?

G   Am7
   I could lose you just like that, may - be forever.

                F   C
There are so many stars. So many stars.

G   Am7   F   C
So many stars.   So many, so many stars.

The Stuff That Dreams Are Made Of

Words and Music by
Carly Simon

Melody:

Take a look a-round now,

Chord diagrams: F, Bb, Bb*, Eb, Ab, Bb/D, C, Am7, G/B, G

Verse 1

F
Take a look around now,

Bb　　　　**F**
　Change the di - rection

Bb　　**F**
　Adjust the tuning,

Bb　　　　**F**
　Try a new trans - lation.

Pre-Chorus 1

　　　Bb*　　　　　　　　　　**Eb**
Don't look at your man in the same old way,

　　　Bb*　　**Eb**
Take a new picture.

　　　Bb*　　　　　　　**Eb**
Just because ____ you don't see shooting stars

　　　　Bb*　　　　**Eb**
Doesn't mean it isn't perfect. Can't you see?

Chorus 1

　　　Ab　　　　　　　**Eb**
It's the stuff that dreams are made ____ of,

　　　Ab　　　　**Eb**
It's the slow and steady fire.

　　　Ab　　　　　　　**Eb**
It's the stuff that dreams are made ____ of,

　　　Ab　　　　　　**Eb**
It's your heart and soul's desire.

　　　Ab　　　　　　**Eb**　　**Bb/D Bb**
It's the stuff that dreams are made ____ of.

Verse 2

       F
So what's this about your best friend?

  Bb   F
   She's got a brand-new shiny boy,

  Bb   F
   And they're moving out to Malibu

  Bb   F
   To play with all his pretty toys.

Pre-Chorus 2

        Bb*   Eb
And you feel closed in by the same four walls,

           Bb* Eb
The same old conver - sation,

        Bb*   Eb
With the same ____ old guy you've known for years.

         Bb*   Eb
But use your imagi - nation and you will see.

Chorus 2

     Ab   Eb
It's the stuff that dreams are made ____ of,

     Ab   Eb
It's the slow and steady fire.

     Ab   Eb
It's the stuff that dreams are made ____ of,

     Ab   Eb
It's your heart and soul's desire.

     Ab   Eb   Bb/D
It's the stuff that dreams are made ____ of.

Bridge

C   Am7
What if the prince on the horse ____ in your fairytale

    G/B   G
Is right ____ here in disguise?

   C   Am7
And what if the stars you've been reach - ing so high for

   G/B   G
Are shining in his eyes?

Verse 3   *Repeat Verse 1 (Instrumental)*

Pre-Chorus 3

        Bb*   Eb

Don't look at yourself in the same old way,

          Bb*   Eb

Take another picture.

             Bb*   Eb

Shoot the stars ___ off in your own backyard,

           Bb*   Eb

Don't look any further and you will see.

Chorus 3

        Ab   Eb

It's the stuff that dreams are made ___ of,

        Ab   Eb

It's the slow and steady fire.

        Ab   Eb

It's the stuff that dreams are made ___ of,

         Ab   Eb

It's your heart and soul's desire.

        Ab   Eb

It's the stuff that dreams are made ___ of,

        Ab   Eb

It's the sails who catch the star.

        Ab   Eb

It's the stuff that dreams are made ___ of,

        Ab   Eb

It's the reason we are alive.

Outro   ‖: Ab | Eb | Ab | Eb   :‖ *Repeat and fade*
                                                     w/ vocal ad lib.

That's the Way I've Always Heard It Should Be

Words and Music by
Carly Simon and Jacob Brackman

Melody:

My fath-er sits at night with no lights on,

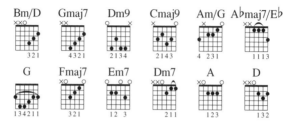

Bm/D   Gmaj7   Dm9   Cmaj9   Am/G   A♭maj7/E♭

G   Fmaj7   Em7   Dm7   A   D

Verse 1

Bm/D   **Gmaj7**
My father sits at night with no lights on,

Bm/D   **Gmaj7**
His cigarette glows in the dark.

Dm9
The living room is still,

Cmaj9   **Am/G**   **A♭maj7/E♭ G**
I walk by no ____ remark.

Bm/D   **Gmaj7**
I tiptoe past the master bedroom

     Bm/D   **Gmaj7**
Where   my mother reads her maga - zines.

Dm9
I hear her call, "Sweet dreams,"

Cmaj9   **Am/G**   **A♭maj7 G**
But I forget how to dream.

Chorus 1

Fmaj7   Em7
But you say it's time we moved in together,

Dm7   Cmaj9
And raised a fam'ly of our own, ___ you and me.

Fmaj7   Em7
Well, that's the way I've always heard it should be.

        A   D
You want to marry me, we'll marry.

Verse 2

Bm/D   Gmaj7
My friends from college, they're all ___ married now.

Bm/D   Gmaj7
They have their houses and their lawns.

Dm9
They have their silent noons,

Cmaj9   Am/G   A♭maj7/E♭ G
Tearful nights, angry ___ dawns.

Bm/D   Gmaj7
Their children hate them for the things they're not.

Bm/D   Gmaj7
They hate themselves for what they ___ are.

Dm9
And yet they drink, they laugh,

Cmaj9   Am/G A♭maj7 G
Close the wound, hide the scar.

Chorus 2   *Repeat Chorus 1*

Verse 3

Bm/D   Gmaj7
You say that we can keep our love alive.

Bm/D   Gmaj7
Babe, all I know is what I see.

Dm9
The couples cling and claw

Cmaj9   Am/G A♭maj7/E♭ G
And drown in love's de - bris.

Bm/D   Gmaj7
You say we'll soar like two birds through the clouds,

Bm/D   Gmaj7
But soon you'll cage me on your shelf.

Dm9
I'll never learn to be

     Cmaj9   Am/G A♭maj7/E♭ G
Just me first, by my - self.

Chorus 3

Fmaj7   Em7
Well, O.K. it's time we moved in together,

Dm7   Cmaj9
And raised a fam'ly of our own, ___ you and me.

Fmaj7   Em7
Well, that's the way I've always heard it should be.

          A   D
You want to marry me, we'll marry.

Time Works on All the Wild Young Men

Words and Music by
Carly Simon and Ben Taylor

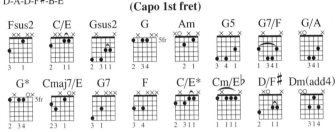

D§ tuning:
(low to high) D-A-D-F♯-B-E

(Capo 1st fret)

Fsus2 C/E Gsus2 G Am G5 G7/F G/A

G* Cmaj7/E G7 F C/E* Cm/E♭ D/F♯ Dm(add4)

Verse

      Fsus2   C/E   Gsus2 G
    Time works on all ____ the wild young men,

        Am   G5
The ones ____ who went for sol - diers,

        G7/F   G/A
The ones who reached for fame,

        Am   G*
The ones ____ who swore they'd die ____ for love

    Cmaj7/E   G/A G7
No mat - ter what the shame.

    F   C/E*   Cm/E♭
    Time circles 'round them, snuffs their spark,

    C/E*   D/F♯ G5   Dm(add4)
And there they are ____ dancing in the dark.

Touched by the Sun

Words and Music by
Carly Simon

Melody:

If you wan-na be brave

G   Bm   A   Em7   D/F#   A/C#

E   C   Asus2   D   G/D

Intro

‖: G | | | |
| Bm | | | A :‖

Verse 1

G
   If you wanna be brave

Bm   A
   And reach for the top of the sky

G   Bm   A
   And the farthest point on the hori - zon,

G
   Do you know who you'll meet there?

   Bm
Great soldiers and seafarers, artists and dreamers

        A   Em7 D/F# G Bm
Who need ____ to be close, close to the light.

      A   Em7 D/F# G Bm
They need to be in danger of burning by fire.

Chorus 1

G   Bm   A
And I, I wanna get there.

G   Bm
I, I wanna be one,

A   Em7 D/F♯
One who is touched by the sun,

A   Em7 D/F♯
One who is touched by the sun,

A   Em7   D/F♯ G Bm A/C♯ D/F♯
One who is touched by ___ the sun.

Verse 2

G
Often I wanna walk

Bm   A
The safe side of the street

  G   Bm   A
And lull myself to sleep and dull my pain. Oh.

G   Bm
But deep down inside I know I've got to learn

From the greats, earn my right to be living,

    A   Em7 D/F♯ G Bm
Let my wings of desire soar over the night.

    A   Em7 D/F♯ G Bm
I need to let them say, "She must have been mad."

Chorus 2

      G Bm   A
And I, I wanna get there.

E G   Bm
I, ___ I wanna be one,

A   Em7 D/F♯
One who is touched by the sun,

A   Em7 D/F♯
One who is touched by the sun,

A   Em7   D/F♯ Bm A/C♯
One who is touched by ___ the sun.

Guitar Solo

G				C Asus2
Bm				A
G				
Bm		A		
Em7	D/F♯	A		
Em7	D/F♯			

Verse 3

      G   Bm
And I've got to learn ___ from the greats,

Earn my right to be living

          A
With ev'ry breath that I take, ev'ry heartbeat.

Outro-Chorus

      G   Bm   A
And I, I wan - na get there.

E G   Bm
I, ___ I wanna be one,

   A   Em7 D/F♯
‖: One who is touched by the sun,   :‖ *Play 5 times*

A   D   G/D D
One who is touched by the sun.

Two Hot Girls (On a Hot Summer Night)

Words and Music by
Carly Simon

Melody:

It hap-pened last night, _ we were feel - ing

C#9sus4 F#9sus4 G#m F# Bmaj9 A6/9

G#m7 F#m/E E B B/D#

Intro

‖: C#9sus4 | | F#9sus4 | :‖

Verse 1

    G#m   F#
It happened last night, we were feeling adven - turous.

    G#m   F#
We put on our heels and went out for a walk.

Bmaj9   A6/9
More for a drink and to have ____ a few eyes on us.

G#m7   F#
Jenny and I slipped to town for some talk.

Chorus 1

F#m/E E   B
Me   and Jenny, twinklin' like crystal and pennies.

   C#9sus4
‖: Two hot girls, on a hot summer night,

F#9sus4
Lookin' for love. :‖

Verse 2

      G#m   F#
Jenny I said, "It's Dwight, he just came ___ in."

      G#m   F#
I got excited but Jenny was quick.

        Bmaj9   A§
The kettle was on and it start - ed up steamin'.

        G#m7   F#
And I knew from her flirtin' she was up to her tricks.

Chorus 2   *Repeat Chorus 1*

Verse 3

       G#m   F#
A song on the jukebox made me feel lone - ly.

       G#m   F#
The kettle boiled down and evaporated me.

        Bmaj9   A§
But who was to notice 'cause Jen - ny was glowin'.

      G#m7   F#
Dwight was all over her like a honeybee.

Chorus 3   *Repeat Chorus 1*

Sax Solo 1   ‖: C#9sus4 | |F#9sus4 | :‖

Verse 4

      G#m   F#
Maybe I shouldn't have worn such a long ___ dress.

      G#m   F#
Maybe he thinks I'm too young or too old.

        Bmaj9   A§
If only I hadn't been born ___ with these sad eyes.

        G#m7   F#
Per - haps I'm too shy or too bold.

Chorus 4

F#/E E   B
Me   and Jenny, twinklin' like crystal and pennies.

   C#9sus4
‖: Two hot girls, on a hot summer night,

F#9sus4
Lookin' for love. :‖

C#9sus4   F#9sus4
Two hot girls.

Verse 5

B   A⅜
Thanks for introduc - ing us,

   G#m7   F#
Said Dwight, polite, and I waved goodnight.

  B/D#   A⅜
I wondered why it was - n't me.

  G#m7   F#
I guess it's just that the time's ___ not right.

Sax Solo 2

Repeat Sax Solo 1

Outro-Chorus

C#9sus4   F#9sus4
Two hot girls.

C#9sus4
Two hot girls, on a hot summer night,

F#9sus4
Lookin' for love.

C#9sus4
Two hot girls, on a hot summer night,

     F#9sus4
They were lookin' for love.

C#9sus4
Two hot girls.

Two Little Sisters

Words and Music by
Carly Simon

Melody:

Two lit - tle sis - ters   gaz-ing at the sea, _____

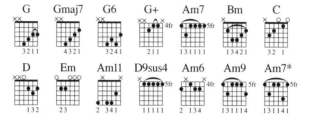

| G | Gmaj7 | G6 | G+ | Am7 | Bm | C |
| D | Em | Am11 | D9sus4 | Am6 | Am9 | Am7* |

Intro

| G Gmaj7 | G6 G+ | G Gmaj7 G6 | G+ G | |

Verse 1

G   Gmaj7 G6   G+ G Gmaj7 G6 G+ G
Two little sisters   gazing at the sea,

        Gmaj7   G6   G+ G Gmaj7 G6 G+ G
Imagining what their futures will be.

   Am7
The older one says, as her eyes look around,

  G   Gmaj7 G6   G+
"I will go as far as the corners of the town.

   Bm
I'll plant a little garden, flowers ev'rywhere.

   C
And pluck the most fragrant for my hair."

G   Gmaj7 G6 G+ G6
Ooh.

G   Gmaj7 G6 G+ G6 G+
Ooh.

Verse 2

G   **Gmaj7 G6**   **G+ G Gmaj7 G6 G+ G**
Two little sisters   gazing at the sea,

       Gmaj7   G6   G+   **G Gmaj7 G6 G+ G**
Imagining what their futures ___ will be.

   Am7
The younger one stands with her eyes open wide

   G   **Gmaj7 G6**   **G+**
And says, "I'll go as far as the corners of the sky.

   Bm
I'll gather all the stars each night as they appear,

   C
And pick the very brightest one to wear in my ear."

G   Gmaj7 G6 G+ G6
  Ooh.

G   Gmaj7 G6 G+ G6 G+
  Ooh.

Bridge

C D   **Em**
I ___ didn't choose you

     D   **Am11 D9sus4 Am11 D9sus4**
And you didn't choose me.

‖: **Am11   D9sus4** :‖

C D   **Em**
I ___ didn't choose you,

      D   **Am11**   **D9sus4 Am11 D9sus4**
Who would guess we're from the same fam - ily?

‖: **Am11   D9sus4** :‖

	G	Gmaj7	G6	G+	G Gmaj7 G6 G+ G

Verse 3   But, what will you do when the nights get cold?

                        Gmaj7   **G6**   **G+ G Gmaj7 G6 G+ G**
When the stars grow dim and your dreams seem old.

Am7   **Am6**   **Am9 Am7 Am7* Am7**
Whacha gonna do when winter calls,

                D
And your flowers fall from the garden walls?

                      G Gmaj7 G6 G+ G
Verse 4   I'll come home to you,

                        Gmaj7 G6 G+ G
You'll come home to me.

           Gmaj7 G6 G+   **G**   **Gmaj7 G6 G+**
My love _____ will be your remedy.

Am7
I'll choose you and you'll choose me.

           D
We'll be two daughters

                    G Gmaj7 G6 G+ G
Dancing by the edge of the sea.

G	Gmaj7 G6	G+	G	

G   Gmaj7 G6   G+ G6
  Ooh.

G   Gmaj7 G6 G+ G6 G+ G
  Ooh, _____ ooh.

Vengeance

Words and Music by
Carly Simon

Melody:

"That's dan-g'rous driv-in', ba-by," the po-lice-man said.

Am   Am7   D7/A   C   D5   E5   Em7   D9   Fmaj7

F#m7b5   E9   Emaj9   C9   Bb9   Bm7   Cmaj7   Fmaj13#11

Intro

| Am | | | |
| | N.C. | Am | |

Verse 1

        Am7   **D7/A**   **Am7**
"That's dang'rous drivin', baby," the po - liceman said.

                               D7/A   **Am7**
"I can smell the passion of another man on your breath.

C   **Am7**   **D5**   **E5**
I could give you life, get you back for what I saw,

      Am7   **Em7**   **Am7**
That's vengeance," he said.   "That's the law."

Chorus 1

        Am7   **D9**
"That's ven - geance. Oh, that's ven - geance.

        Fmaj7
Yeah, that's ven - geance," he said.

Em7   **Am7**
   "That's the law. That's vengeance.

       D9   **Fmaj7**
Oh, that's ven - geance. Yeah that's ven - geance," he said.

Em7   **Am7** N.C.
   "That's the law."

Verse 2

     Am7   D7/A   Am7
"You throw your misdemeanors right up in my face.

               D7/A   Am7
The kind of man I am I got to put you in your place.

C   Am7   D5   E5
I should lock you up; get you back for what I saw.

    Am7   Em7   Am7
That's vengeance," he said. "That's the law."

Chorus 2   *Repeat Chorus 1*

Bridge

    F♯m7♭5
You've taken your half out of the middle,

     E9   Emaj9
Oh, time ____ and time again.

      D9
But now I'm damned if I'll give you an inch

     C9   B♭9
Till I get e - ven.

Guitar Solo | Am7 | Bm7 Cmaj7 | Am7 | Bm7 Cmaj7 |

        | Am7 | Bm7 Cmaj7 | Fmaj13♯11 D5 |

Verse 3

Em7   Am7   D7/A   Am7
 She said, "Just because you're stronger and you hold it over me,

               D7/A   Am7
I'll put the pedal to the floor and prove to you that I'm free.

      C   Am7   D5   E5
Though you stopped me once a - gain, it's not the end of the war.

    Am7   Em7   Am7
It's vengeance," she said "That's the law."

| *Chorus 3* | Am7   D9 |

Am7   **D9**

Chorus 3   "That's ven - geance. Oh, that's ven - geance.

                  Fmaj7

Yeah, that's ven - geance," she said.

Em7   **Am7**

  "That's the law. That's vengeance.

                  D9   **Fmaj7**

Yeah, yeah, that's ven - geance. Well, that's ven - geance," she said.

Em7   **Am7** N.C.

  "That's the law."

Interlude | **Am7** | **N.C.(Am)** | | |

  Vengeance.

| | | | **Em7** **Am7** |

Am7   **D9**

Outro-Chorus   "That's ven - geance. Yeah, that's ven - geance.

                  Fmaj7

Oh, that's ven - geance," she said.

Em7   **Am7**

  "That's the law. That's vengeance.

                  D9   **Fmaj7**

Yeah, sweet ___ vengeance. Yeah that's ven - geance," she said.

Em7   **Am7** N.C.

  "That's the law."

      Am7   **D9**

"Ven - geance, oh, that's ven - geance.

                  Fmaj7

Yeah, that's ven - geance," she said.

Em7   **Am7**

  "That's the law."

                  D9

"Vengeance, yeah, yeah, ven - geance.

                  Fmaj7

Yeah, that's ven - geance," she said.

Em7   **Am7**

  "That's the law."

Whatever Became of Her

Words and Music by
Carly Simon

Melody:

There they are,   smil-ing so

Bm11   Asus2   E   Asus2*   Bsus4   C#m   G#m7   D   A   F#m7

B   Em7   G   F#7   Bm   C#m7   F#m   F   Fsus2

Intro   ‖: **Bm11** | **Asus2**   :‖   ***Play 4 times***

Verse 1

            E   **Asus2***
There they are,

Bsus4   **E**
Smiling so wide

         C#m   **G#m7**
Like there's nothing to lose

      D   **A**
And nothing to hide.

           E   **Asus2***
They look forward with innocence.

Bsus4   **E**
She is his bride,

      C#m   **G#m7** **A** **Asus2*** **A** **Asus2***
The future's a radiant blur.

Chorus 1

         F#m7   **B**   **Em7**   **A**
So, I wonder what - ever be - came of him.

        G   **F#7**   **Bm**   **Asus2*** **Bm** **Asus2***
What - ever be - came of ____ her?

Verse 2

        E   Asus2*
A little boutique

        Bsus4   E
On the Upper East Side,

C#m   G#m7 D   Asus2*
Picture a cou - ple so dignified.

       E   Asus2*
Two hat boxes fall

       Bsus4   E
And feathers collide;

        C#m7   G#m7   A Asus2* A
Darling tell me, which one ___ do you prefer?

Chorus 2

        F#m7   B   Em7   A
Well, I wonder what - ever be - came of ___ him.

       G   F#7   Bm11 Asus2
What - ever be - came of her?

Bridge 1

D   E   F#m   A
Ev'rything breaks ___ except the broken plates.

D   E   F#m   F
Ev'rything gets stolen except the things you don't want anyway.

    F#m   F   Fsus2
The things you don't want an - yway.

Verse 3

E   Asus2*
She played the piano

    Bsus4   E
And he used to smoke.

       C#m   G#m7   D   A
She used to slap her own thigh ___ when he made a joke.

      E   Asus2*
He started her heart

     Bsus4   E
When - ever he spoke,

C#m   G#m7   A   Asus2* A
His own turning cold, like a bird.

                    F#m7   B   Em7   A
Chorus 3   Well, I wonder what - ever be - came of him.

                         G   F#7   Bm   Asus2* Bm Asus2*
                    What - ever be - came of ___ her?

                    D   E   F#m   A
Bridge 2   I wanna say, "No,   go back, ___ resist.

                         D   E
                    Don't step out of the photograph,

                    F#m   F
                    Don't hurt yourselves, stay innocent.

                    F#m   F Fsus2 F Fsus2
                    Don't hurt yourselves."

                    E   Asus2*
Verse 4   Two shadows playing

                    Bsus4   E
                      Across the lawn.

                         C#m   G#m7 D   Asus2*
                    Is it to - morrow's twilight ___ or yesterday's dawn?

                         E   Asus2*
                    You can hardly make out

                    Bsus4   E
                    What they've got on

                         C#m   G#m7   A Asus2* A Asus2*
                    But they're mighty in love, ___ you'll agree.

                         F#m7   B   Em7   A Asus2* A Asus2*
Chorus 4   So, I wonder what - ever be - came of him.

                         G   F#7   Bm11   Asus2
                    What - ever be - came of ___ me?

Outro   ‖: Bm11   │Asus2   :‖ *Repeat and fade*

You Belong to Me

Words and Music by
Carly Simon and Michael McDonald

Melody:

Why'd you tell me this? Were you

Fm9 G7sus4 Cm9 Abmaj7 G+/B Cm7 Ebmaj7 Eb7

Eb/F F6 Abmaj7/Bb C7#5 Bbm7 Fm7 C7sus4

Dm7b5 Dbmaj7 C7 Bb7sus4 Bb13 Eb9 Gm7b5

Intro

‖: Fm9 | G7sus4 | Cm9 | | :‖

Verse 1

        Fm9
Why'd you tell me this?

      G7sus4   **Cm9**
Were you looking for my ___ reaction?

        Fm9
What do you need to know?

       G7sus4   **Cm9**
Don't you know ___ I'll always be ___ your girl?

Pre-Chorus 1

       Abmaj7
You don't have to prove to me

      G7sus4 **G+/B**   **Cm7**
You're beau - tiful _____ to strang - ers.

   Ebmaj7 **Eb7**   **Eb/F** **F6**
I've ___ got loving eyes

 Eb/F **F6**   **Abmaj7/Bb**
Of my ___ own.

Copyright © 1977 C'est Music and Snug Music
Copyright Renewed
All Rights for C'est Music Administered by BMG Rights Management (US) LLC
All Rights for Snug Music Administered by Wixen Music Publishing, Inc.
All Rights Reserved   Used by Permission

Chorus 1

G7sus4 C7#5   B♭m7
(You belong to me.) Tell her, tell her you were foolin'.

Fm7
(You belong to me.) You don't even know her.

B♭m7
(You belong to me.) Tell her that I love you.

C7sus4 C7#5
(You belong to me.)

Verse 2

Fm9
You belong ___ to me.

G7sus4   Cm9
Can it be that you're not sure?

Fm9
You belong to me.

G7sus4   Cm9
Thought we'd closed the book an' locked ___ the door.

Pre-Chorus 2

A♭maj7
You don't have to prove to me

G7sus4 G+/B   Cm7
That you're beau - tiful _____ to strang - ers.

E♭maj7 E♭7   E♭/F   F6
I've ___ got loving eyes ___ of my own,

E♭/F F6   A♭maj7/B♭   G7sus4
Of my _____ own and I ___ can tell, I can tell darling,

Chorus 2

Dm7♭5 C7♯5   B♭m7
Tell _____ her, tell her that I love you.

Fm7
(You belong to me.) I've known you from a long time ago, baby.

B♭m7
(You belong to me.) Tell her you were foolin'.

Fm7
(You belong to me.) Tell her she don't even know you.

Sax Solo

|Dbmaj7 |C7sus4   C7 |Fm7 |Abmaj7 |

|Bb7sus4 Bb13 |Bb7sus4 Bb13 |Eb9 |

Chorus 3

Gm7♭5 C7♯5 B♭m7
Tell   her, tell her you were foolin'.

Fm7
(You belong to me.) You belong, you belong, you belong to me.

B♭m7
(You belong to me.) Tell her that I love you.

Fm7
(You belong to me.) 'Cause you belong to me, baby.

Outro

B♭m7   Fm7
‖: (You belong to me. You belong to me.) :‖ *Repeat and fade*
                                               w/ lead vocal ad lib.

You're So Vain

Words and Music by
Carly Simon

Melody:

You walked in - to the par - ty

Am7	F	Fmaj7	G	Em7	C

Dm7	Am	G13	Asus2	G7	Em

Intro

| N.C.(Am) | | Am7 | | |
| | | | | |

Verse 1

       Am7
You walked into the party

             F   **Fmaj7 F**   **Am7**
Like you were walking on - to   a yacht.

Your hair strategic'lly dipped below one eye,

       F   **Fmaj7 F**   **Am7**
Your scarf, it was apri - cot.

      Fmaj7 G   **Em7**
You had one eye in the mir - ror

Am7 F   **C**
As you watched yourself gavotte.

           G   **F**
And all the girls dreamed that they'd be your partner,

They'd be your partner, and…

Chorus 1

      C   Dm7   C
You're so vain, you prob'bly think this song is a - bout you.

              Am
You're so vain, ___ (You're so vain.)

      Fmaj7   G13
I'll bet you think this song is about ___ you.

Don't you, don't you?

Verse 2

           Am7
Oh, you had me sev'ral years ago,

        F   Fmaj7 F   Am7
When I was still quite   naïve.

Well, you said that we made such a pretty pair

       F   Fmaj7 F   Am7
And that you would nev - er leave.

       Fmaj7 G   Em7   Am7
But you gave a - way the things you loved,

       F   C
And one of them was me.

          G   F
I had some dreams, they were clouds in my coffee,

Clouds in my coffee, and…

Chorus 2

      C   Dm7   C
You're so vain, you prob'bly think this song is a - bout you.

              Am
You're so vain, ___ (You're so vain.)

      Fmaj7   G13
I'll bet you think this song is about ___ you.

Don't you, don't you, don't you?

Guitar Solo
```
|Am7 Am Am7 |   Am   |F  Fmaj7 |Am Asus2 Am7 |
|    Am    |Am7 Am |F   Am |   Asus2    |
|Fmaj7 G7  |Em   Am |F       |
```

C   G   F
I had some dreams, they were clouds in my coffee,

Clouds in my coffee, and…

Chorus 3   *Repeat Chorus 1*

                Am7
Verse 3   Well, I hear you went up to Saratoga,

        F   Fmaj7 F   Am7
And your horse ___ na - t'rally won.

Then you flew your Lear jet up to Nova Scotia

               F   Fmaj7 F   Am7
To see the total e - clipse of the sun.

              Fmaj7   G   Em7 Am7
Well, you're where you should be all the time,

        F   C   G
And when you're not, you're with ___ some underworld spy

        F
Or the wife of a close friend, wife of a close friend, and…

Chorus 4   *Repeat Chorus 2*

Interlude
```
|C     |     |Dm7  |C    |
```

            C   Dm7
Outro   **||:** You're so vain, you prob'bly think

                      C
This song is about __ you. **:||** *Repeat and fade*

Guitar Chord Songbooks

Each book includes complete lyrics, chord symbols, and guitar chord diagrams.

FOR MORE INFORMATION, SEE YOUR LOCAL MUSIC DEALER,
OR WRITE TO:

HAL•LEONARD®
CORPORATION
7777 W. BLUEMOUND RD. P.O. BOX 13819 MILWAUKEE, WI 53213

Visit Hal Leonard online at
www.halleonard.com

Prices, contents, and availability subject to change without notice.

1013